J. H. Kurzenknabe

Silvery Echoes of Praise and Prayer

a collection of hymns and music, especially adapted for children and youth

in the primary and intermediate Departments of the Sunday-School

J. H. Kurzenknabe

Silvery Echoes of Praise and Prayer
a collection of hymns and music, especially adapted for children and youth in the primary and intermediate Departments of the Sunday-School

ISBN/EAN: 9783337089542

Printed in Europe, USA, Canada, Australia, Japan

Cover: Foto ©Lupo / pixelio.de

More available books at **www.hansebooks.com**

OF

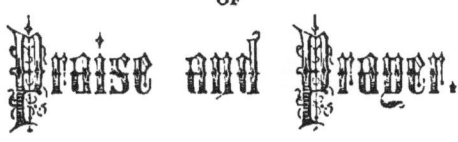

COLLECTION OF HYMNS AND MUSIC,

ESPECIALLY ADAPTED FOR

CHILDREN AND YOUTHS

IN THE

Primary and Intermediate Departments

OF THE

SUNDAY-SCHOOL.

BY

J. H. KURZENKNABE.

AUTHOR OF "SONG TREASURY," "THE REWARD," "NEW THEORY."

PUBLISHED BY

CRIDER & BROTHER:

YORK, PENNSYLVANIA.

Single Copy, Post-paid, 25cts. By Express, $2.40 per Dozen; $20.00 per 100.

[Copyright, 1880, by CRIDER & BRO.]

PREFACE.

"SILVERY ECHOES" is designed to fill the place in the Primary and Intermediate Departments of the Sunday-school similar to that now occupied by the "SONG TREASURY" in the Main School. Hence the two go hand in hand on their mission of praise.

May its happy sonnets vibrate throughout the land in universal praise, until, in silvery echoes, they reach the Hills of Eternity in adoration of Him who is worthy to receive "power, and riches, and wisdom, and strength, and honor, and glory, and blessing" forever and ever! Amen.

, J. H. KURZENKNABE.

The following will aid in the selection of suitable topics for desired occasions:—
Praise. 3, 4, 6, 11, 18, 20, 21, 24, 31, 37, 43, 44, 45, 51, 53, 63, 64, 68, 72, 79.
Prayer. 7, 10, 12, 13, 14, 16, 17, 23, 26, 27, 28, 29, 32, 33, 34, 39, 46, 48, 55, 61, 70, 75.
Christian Life and Experience. 8, 21, 25, 26, 35, 42, 48, 49, 50, 57, 74, 76.
Childhood and Youth. 3, 5, 12, 17, 21, 28, 35, 38, 42, 44, 47, 51, 58, 62, 68, 74, 75.
Saviour's Love. 7, 8, 18, 34, 44, 54, 61, 72, 76.
Sabbath School. 9, 27, 46, 62, 78.
Heaven and Home. 15, 36, 41, 50, 52.
Coming to Jesus. 19, 25, 40, 47, 57.
Invitation. 36, 42, 50, 52.
Children's Shepherd. 22, 30, 75.
Children's Saviour. 16, 53, 54, 57, 60, 76.
Warfare. 5, 38, 49, 58.
Solos. 9, 30, 34, 40, 58, 60, 72, 76.
Duets. 5, 7, 33, 47, 50.
Trios, Echoes, Chants, and Lullaby. 4, 11, 63, 73, 79.
Christmas. 53, 64, 65.
Anniversaries, Concerts, etc. 4, 5, 6, 7, 9, 11, 17, 20, 24, 27, 30, 33, 34, 36, 37, 38, 40, 44, 47, 49, 50, 51, 52, 54, 56, 57, 58, 60, 63, 66, 68, 70, 72, 74, 76, 78, 79.

SPECIAL NOTICE.

Any person printing the copyright words or music contained in this book, without the written permission of the author or publishers, will be held amenable for violation of the copyright law.

SILVERY ECHOES.

WE PRAISE THEE, LORD.

G. GESSNER. H. G. NAGELL.

1 We praise thee, Lord, In childhood's hap-py morn-ing,
2 In joy-ful strain, With youthful voic-es blend-ing,
3 With hearts a-glow, We sing the sim-ple sto-ry,
4 We glad-ly raise The an-them of sal-va-tion,

In sweet ac-cord Thy love our hearts a-dorn-ing,
In glad re-frain To heav-en now as-cend-ing.
And prais-es, too, Of Je-sus and his glo-ry.
To crown our praise With fer-vent ad-o-ra-tion.

CHORUS.

We praise thee, Lord, We praise thee, Lord.

LITTLE PILGRIMS.

LIZZIE ASHBAUGH. (Marching Song.) J. H. KURZENKNABE.

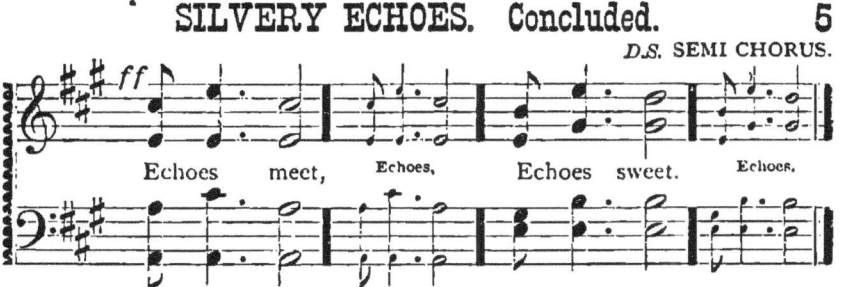

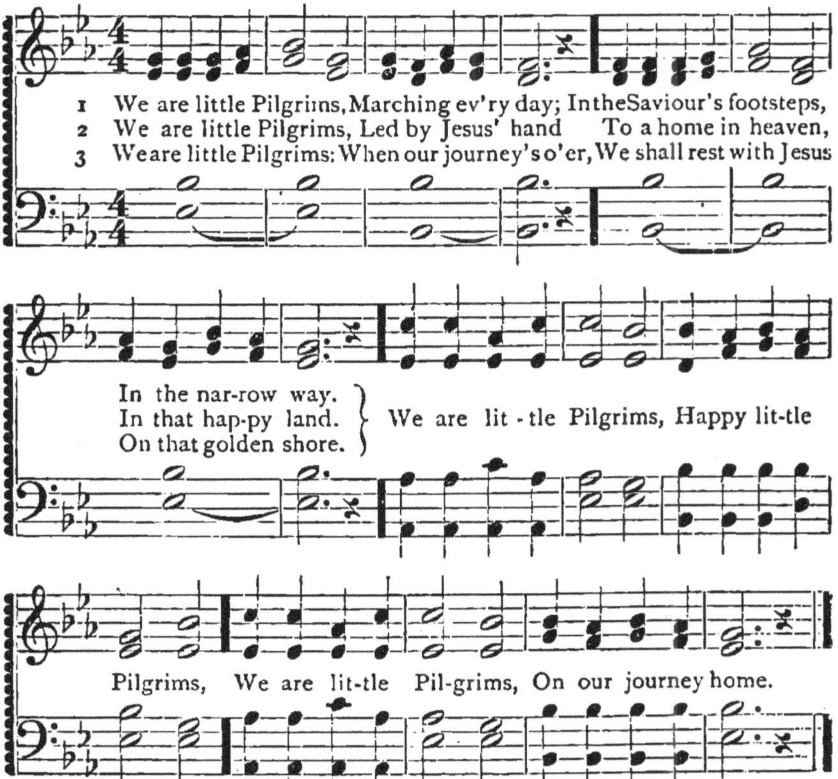

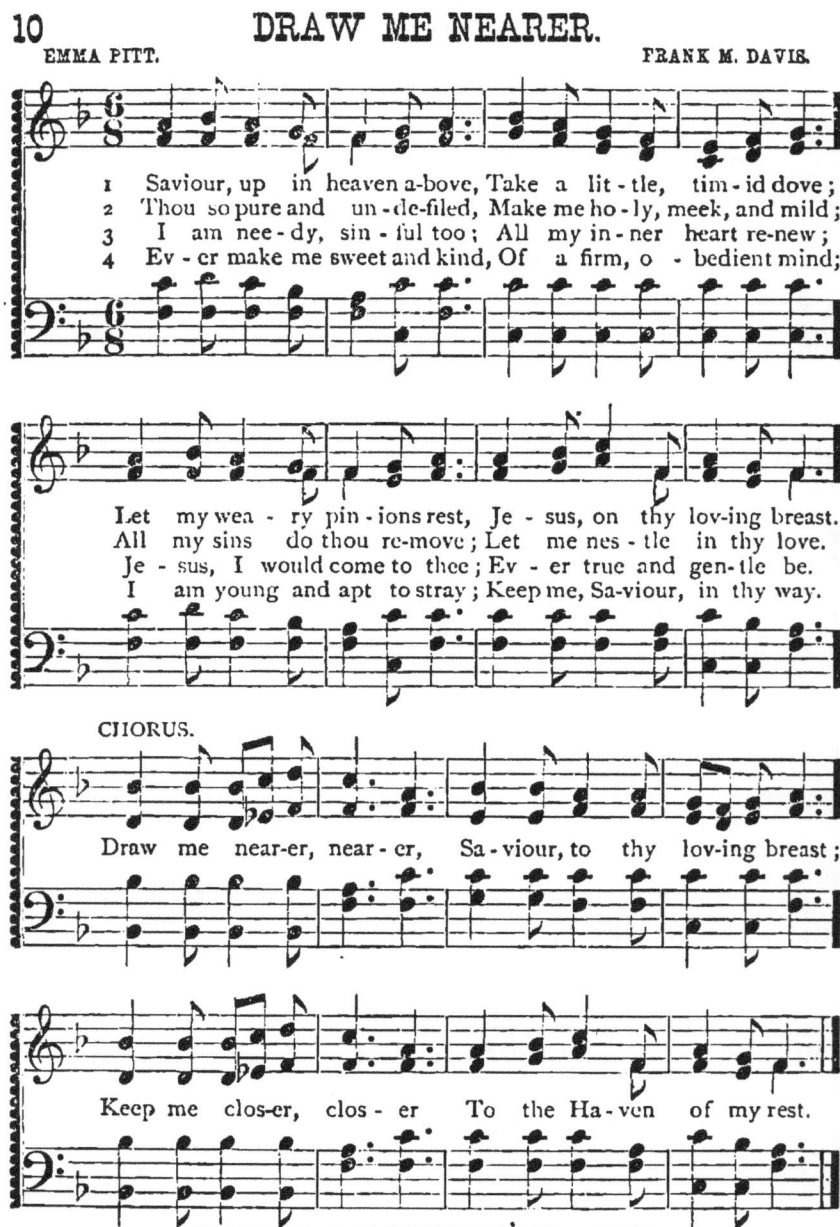

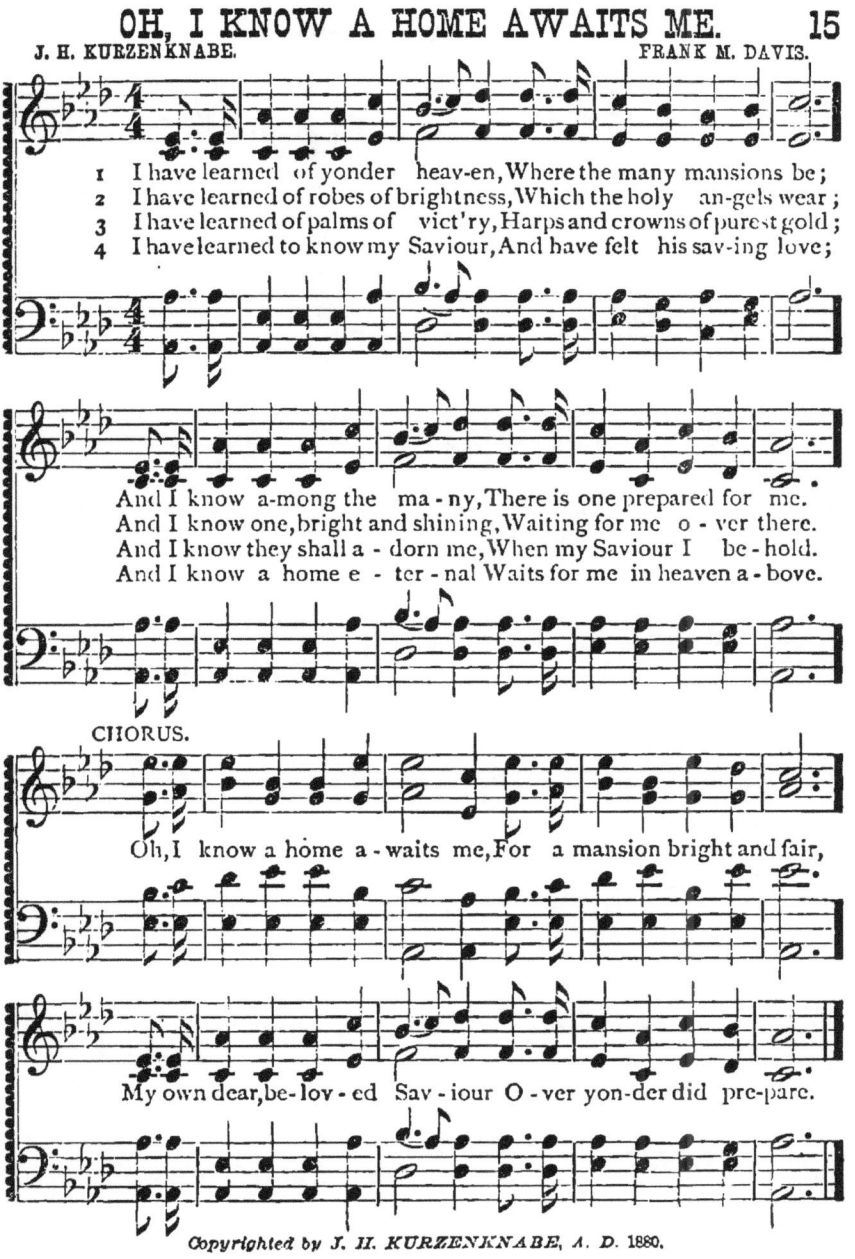

16. NEARER TO THEE, BLESSED SAVIOUR.

J. H. KURZENKNABE. JNO. R. SWENEY.

1. Near-er to thee, bless-ed Saviour, To thy embraces we flee;
2. Near-er to thee, bless-ed Saviour, Thy sweetest smiles to receive,
3. Near-er to thee, bless-ed Saviour, Thy little children would hide:
4. Near-er to thee, bless-ed Saviour, Near-er to thy tender breast.

Grant lit-tle children a re-fuge, Grant us a shel-ter in thee.
We, like the faint droop-ing lil-ies, Need brightest sunshine to live.
We are so frail and so err-ing; Take us with thee to a-bide.
Hear us, thou Friend of the children; Grant us our humble re-quest.

CHORUS.

Near-er, near-er, near-er, bless-ed Saviour, to thee,
Near-er, near-er, near-er, bless-ed Sav-iour, to thee.

Copyrighted by J. H. KURZENKNABE, A. D. 1880.

HAPPY IN THE LORD.

J. H. K.
J. H. KURZENKNABE.

1. Lit-tle chil-dren come to-day, Hap-py in the Lord;
2. Je-sus loves to hear our praise, Hap-py in the Lord;
3. By the Saviour's pard'ning blood, Hap-py in the Lord;
4. Then when done with mor-tal praise, Hap-py in the Lord;

D. C. Lit-tle chil-dren come to-day, Hap-py in the Lord.

We u-nite to sing and pray, Hap-py in the Lord.
He will keep us all our days, Hap-py in the Lord.
We are cleansed from ev'-ry spot, Hap-py in the Lord.
We shall wor-ship face to face, Hap-py in the Lord.

We u-nite to sing and pray, Hap-py in the Lord

CHORUS.

Here with tune-ful voic-es All in sweet ac-cord;

D.C.

Ev-'ry one re-joic-es, Hap-py in the Lord.

Copyrighted by J. H. KURZENKNABE, A.D. 1880.

OH, GRANT US NOW THY PRESENCE.

Selected. *Earnestly.*   Arr. from the German.

1 To thee, our heavenly Father, Our grate-ful songs we raise,
With glad-some hearts and voices, Thy ho - ly name to praise.
2 We bring our hearts an off'ring To thee, our Sa - viour King.
Teach us, thou dear Re-deem-er, Thy prais - es here to sing.

3 Oh, guide us, bless - ed Spir - it, And grant us heavenly food;
So that the Ho - ly Scriptures By us be un - derstood.
4 O Fa - ther, Son, and Spir - it, Thrice blessed Three in One,
Grant us that we in - her- it The king-dom, all thine own.

CHORUS.

Oh, grant us now thy presence, While we to-day have come
To wor - ship thee to-geth-er In our dear Sabbath home.

TEACH US MORE OF THEE. 29

May we ev-er, may we ev-er Rev'rent in thy courts ap-pear.
Lov-ing Sa-viour, lov-ing Sa-viour, In thine arms, oh, may we rest.
Oh, for-ev-er and for-ev-er, Ev-er-more to dwell with thee.

THOU GOD OF LOVE AND MERCY, HEAR.

Selected.   Dr. MARTIN LUTHER.

1 Thou God of love and mer-cy, hear Our grate-ful vows and fer-vent prayer; And with thy choic-est fa-vors bless, And own as thine the ris-ing race.
2 In-cline our hearts to learn thy will; Our open-ing minds with knowledge fill; Im-press thine im-age on our breast, And guide us to thine heavenly rest.
3 Lord, oh, ac-cept our soul's de-sire, And let us nev-er faint nor tire From walk-ing in thy sa-cred ways, And give us strength to live thy praise.

THE CHILDREN'S SHEPHERD.

watch-ful-ly lead them, And quiet their fears under ev'-ry a-larm.
search ev'-ry byway, And listen un-til he shall hear its faint bleat.
ev-er befriend them, Till all are safe housed in his bright home above.

OH, FOR A HEART TO PRAISE.

Rev. J. H. MILLET.

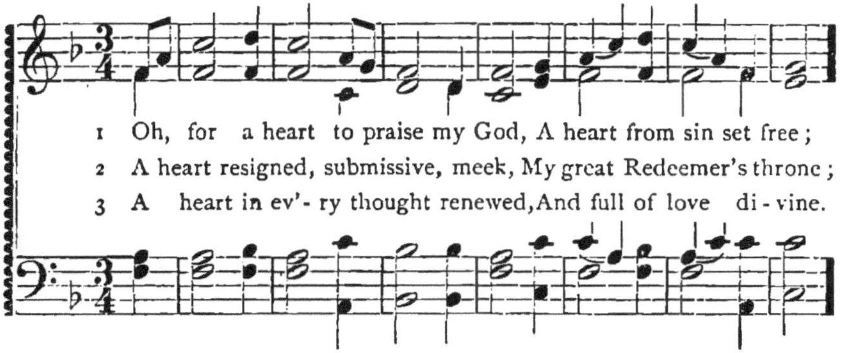

1 Oh, for a heart to praise my God, A heart from sin set free;
2 A heart resigned, submissive, meek, My great Redeemer's throne;
3 A heart in ev'-ry thought renewed, And full of love di-vine.

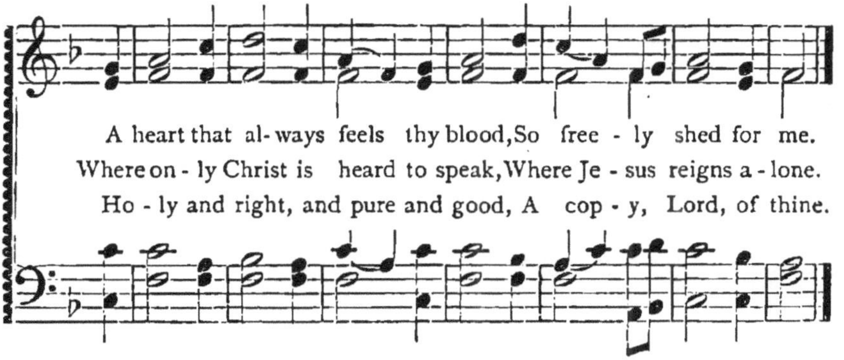

A heart that al-ways feels thy blood, So free-ly shed for me.
Where on-ly Christ is heard to speak, Where Je-sus reigns a-lone.
Ho-ly and right, and pure and good, A cop-y, Lord, of thine.

40. LET THEM COME UNTO ME.

Rev. P. S. ORWIG.   D. F. HODGES.

SOLO. *Semplice.*

1. We chil-dren now do glad-ly come To thee, dear Lord, to-day;
2. Thou art the children's Friend to-day, Just like in days of old;
3. We need not fear, but boldly come To thee, and learn of thee;

We know that thou for us hast room, For thou thyself didst say.
And wilt not turn a child a-way, But take it in thy fold.
And none can keep us from our home, Where thou wilt, we would be.

CHORUS.
soli.   *tutti.*   *soli.*   *tutti.*

Let them come, let them come Un-to me; let them come

Copyrighted by J. H. KURZENKNABE, A. D. 1880.

LET THEM COME UNTO ME.

Un-to me, and forbid them not, For of such is the kingdom of heaven.

THE HAPPY LAND.

LIZZIE ASHBAUGH.
German Melody.

1 Would you reach that heavenly land,
  Where the saints in glo-ry stand,
2 There with-in that hap-py land,
  We shall walk the golden strand,
3 Ours shall be that hap-py land,
  Guard-ed by our Father's hand,

Ev-er and for-ev-er.

D.C. While the heavenly song shall ring,
D.C. And a mansion have with-in,
D.C. And for-ev-er hap-py be,

Ever and for-ev-er.

Would you with them sweetly sing, Prais-es to the Sa-viour King,
Strive if you would en-ter in, There a crown of glo-ry win,
When from sin and sor-row free, We shall our dear Sa-viour see,

42. CALLING, GENTLY CALLING.

Rev. J. M. LYONS.   JNO. J. HOOD.

1. In the midnight si-lent watches, What a wondrous voice I hear!
2. Blessed Lord, O great Cre-a-tor, How I won-der can it be,
3. There again I hear thee call-ing, In such tender accents near;
4. Speak, O Lord, thy servant heareth; Help thou me to understand;

Charming accents, sweet and tender, Music-like, salute mine ear.
He that built the star-ry mansion, Doth re-gard a child like me.
Here am I! oh, yes, I lis-ten; Speak, and I will gladly hear.
Here I wait to do thy er-rands, And obey, Lord, thy command.

CHORUS.

Call-ing, gen-tly call - ing, Wondrous accents, sweet and mild,

Call - ing, for he loves me; He loves a lit - tle child.

Copyrighted by J. H. KURZENKNABE, A.D. 1880.

OH, WE ARE WELCOME.

J. H. KURZENKNABE. J. B. MURRAY.

1 Lord, we come; thy lit-tle children Know in thy arms still is room;
2 Suf-fer them, how ver-y precious; Blessed Sa-viour, we are here;
3 Suf-fer them, oh, words so tender; In thine arms and by thy side
4 In thy steps we'll try to fol-low, Wander nev-er more astray,

None dare keep us from thy presence Thou'st said, suffer them to come.
At thy word we glad-ly hasten'd, For a blessing waits us there.
There is refuge, there is shelter, From life's storms and raging tide.
And in yonder heavenly kingdom We shall be with thee for aye.

CHORUS.

Suffer them: oh, we are welcome, Though the world may scorn or frown;

Welcome to thy blessed ser-vice, Welcome to a starry crown.

Copyrighted by J. H. KURZENKNABE, A. D. 1880.

TAKE HIM AT HIS WORD. 57

Mrs. J. H. WITMAN.   J. H. KURZENKNABE.

1 Je-sus says, come un-to me; Let us take him at his word;
2 Closely fold-ed to his arms, He will keep us day by day;
3 Yet to-day, as when of old, Shall each lit-tle lamb be blest;
4 Saviour, here we come to thee; Help us wor-ship at thy feet;

Oh, how hap-py we shall be To be with the blessed Lord.
Here no fears and no a-larms Can o'er-take us by the way.
And with-in his ten-der fold All may safe-ly, sweet-ly rest.
To thy lov-ing arms we flee; Make our hap-pi-ness complete.

CHORUS.

With-out a doubt, with-out a fear, Take him at his word;

With-out a doubt, with-out a fear, Take him at his word.

Copyrighted by J. H. KURZENKNABE, A. D. 1880.

58. THE CAPTAIN'S BAND.

VERSE 1.—A little boy marches to front of stage singing:—Standard, *Immanuel*. In chorus, march to opposite side in semicircle, and return. VERSE 2. Second boy joins first boy:—Standard, *Red Cross in white field*. Join in chorus, march. VERSE 3.—Third boy advances:—Standard, *Open Bible*. Joins first two in chorus, when a company of little soldiers advance to martial music, and, singing, join in march around stage. VERSE 4.—Face the audience, kneel in last two lines, rise in chorus, and while singing and with drums beating, march off stage.

J. H. K. J. H. KURZENKNABE.

1. I'm a Christian soldier, standing for the right;
2. Faithful little soldier, I would enter here;
3. Pass the word attention all along the line;
4. Hear the cry of woe that falls upon the ear;

Though I am but small, I'll battle with my might;
For I love to be a gallant volunteer;
Ev'ry soldier ready and in marching time;
Satan's host advances from afar and near;

My beloved Captain has accepted me,
I have heard the call and valiantly I'll stand,
At the order—Forward, let each trusty man
Oh, thou heavenly Father, we would humbly beg,

Copyrighted by J. H. KURZENKNABE, A. D. 1880.

THE CHILDREN'S SAVIOUR.

Rev. J. B. ATCHINSON. J. H. KURZENKNABE.

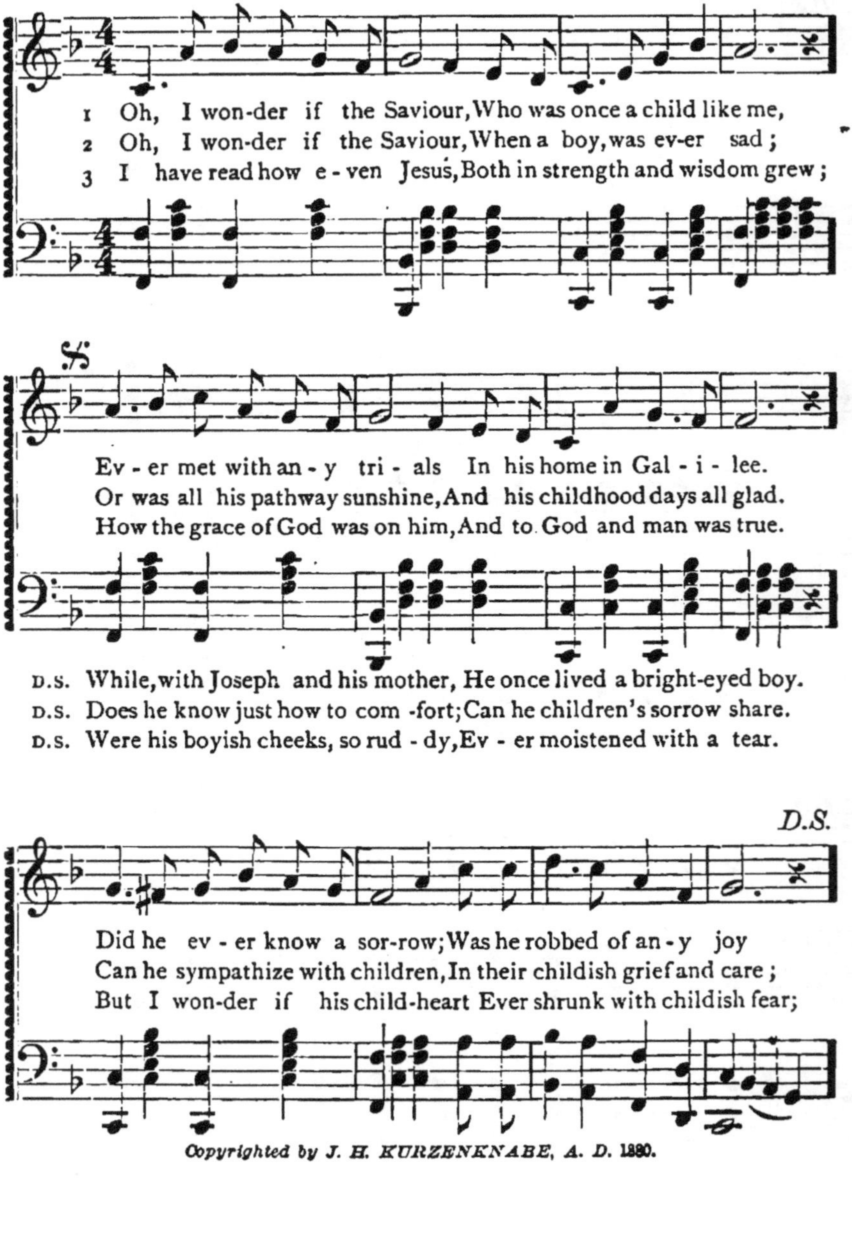

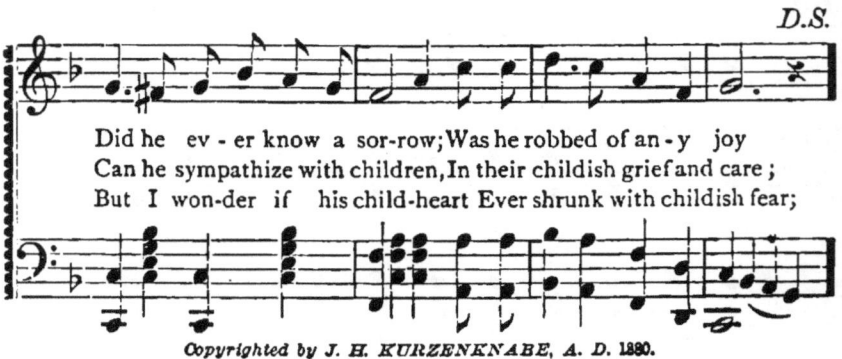

THE CHILDREN'S SAVIOUR.

Chorus after each D.S.

Yes, oh, yes, the children's Saviour Has felt ev'-ry child-ish grief;

For in all points he was tempted, And knows how to give re-lief.

JESUS, THE VERY THOUGHT OF THEE.

N. HERMAN. 1560.

1. Je-sus, the ver-y thought of thee, With sweetness fills my breast;
2. No voice can sing, no heart can frame, Nor can the memory find,
3. Oh, hope of ev'-ry con-trite heart, Oh, joy of all the meek,
4. How sweet thy love, dear Sa-viour, this No tongue nor pen can show;

Repeat pp.

But sweet-er far thy face to see, And in thy presence rest.
A sweet-er sound than Je-sus' name, The Saviour of man-kind.
To err-ing ones how kind thou art! How good to those who seek!
The love of Je-sus, what it is, None but the loved ones know.

Recitation [*after the singing of second verse,*] by Superintendent and sixteen little scholars, each bringing up a letter and handing it to Superintendent, who places the same on a wire, stretched across the pulpit recess.

Supt. Charity suffereth long.
1st Scholar Advances. And above all things have fervent charity among yourselves, for charity shall cover a multitude of sins.—Peter iv. 8.
Supt. And is kind.
2d Scholar. Add to goodness brotherly kindness, and to brotherly kindness charity.—2 Peter i. 7.

Copyrighted by J. H. KURZENKNABE, A. D. 1880.

CHARITY.

Supt. Charity envieth not.
3d Scholar. Hatred stirreth up strifes; but love covereth all sins.—Prov. x. 12.

Supt. Vaunteth not itself.
4th Scholar. Look not every man on his own things, but every man also on the things of others.—Phil. ii. 4.

Supt. Is not puffed up.
5th Scholar. Knowledge puffeth up; but charity edifieth.—1 Cor. viii. 1.

Supt. Doth not behave itself unseemly.
6th Scholar. Be thou an example of the believers in word, in conversation, in charity, in spirit, in faith, in purity.—1 Tim. iv. 12.

Supt. Seeketh not her own.
7th Scholar. Let no man seek his own, but every man another's wealth.—1 Cor. x. 24.

Supt. Is not easily provoked.
8th Scholar. And the servant of the Lord must not strive; but be gentle unto all men, apt to teach, patient. 2 Tim. ii. 24.

Supt. Thinketh no evil.
9th Scholar. Follow after charity, and desire spiritual gifts.—1 Cor. xii 1.

Supt. Rejoiceth not in iniquity.
10th Scholar. We that are strong ought to bear the infirmities of the weak.—Rom. xv. 1.

Supt. But rejoiceth in the truth.
11th Scholar. I rejoice greatly that I found of thy children walking in truth, as we have received a commandment from the Father.—2 John 4.

Supt. Beareth all things.
12th Scholar. Bear ye one another's burden, and so fulfil the law of Christ.—Gal. vi. 2.

Supt. Believeth all things.
13th Scholar. Now the end of all is charity, out of a pure heart, and of a good conscience, and a faith unfeigned.—1 Tim. i. 5.

Supt. Hopeth all things.
14th Scholar. Which hope we have as an anchor of the soul, both sure and steadfast, and which entereth into that within the vail.—Heb. vi. 19.

Supt. Endureth all things.
15th Scholar. And above all things, put on charity, which is the bond of perfectness.—Col. iii. 14.

Supt. Charity never faileth.
16th Scholar. Let all your things be done with charity.—1 Cor. xvi. 14.

School sing third and fourth verses, after which Superintendent recites as follows:

CHRISTIAN GRACES.	EMBLEMS.
Supt. { And now abideth Faith, Hope, Charity, These three, but the greatest of these is Charity.	1st Little boy plants a Cross on a mound. 2d Little boy fastens an Anchor to base of Cross. 3d Little boy fastens a Heart on breast of Cross.

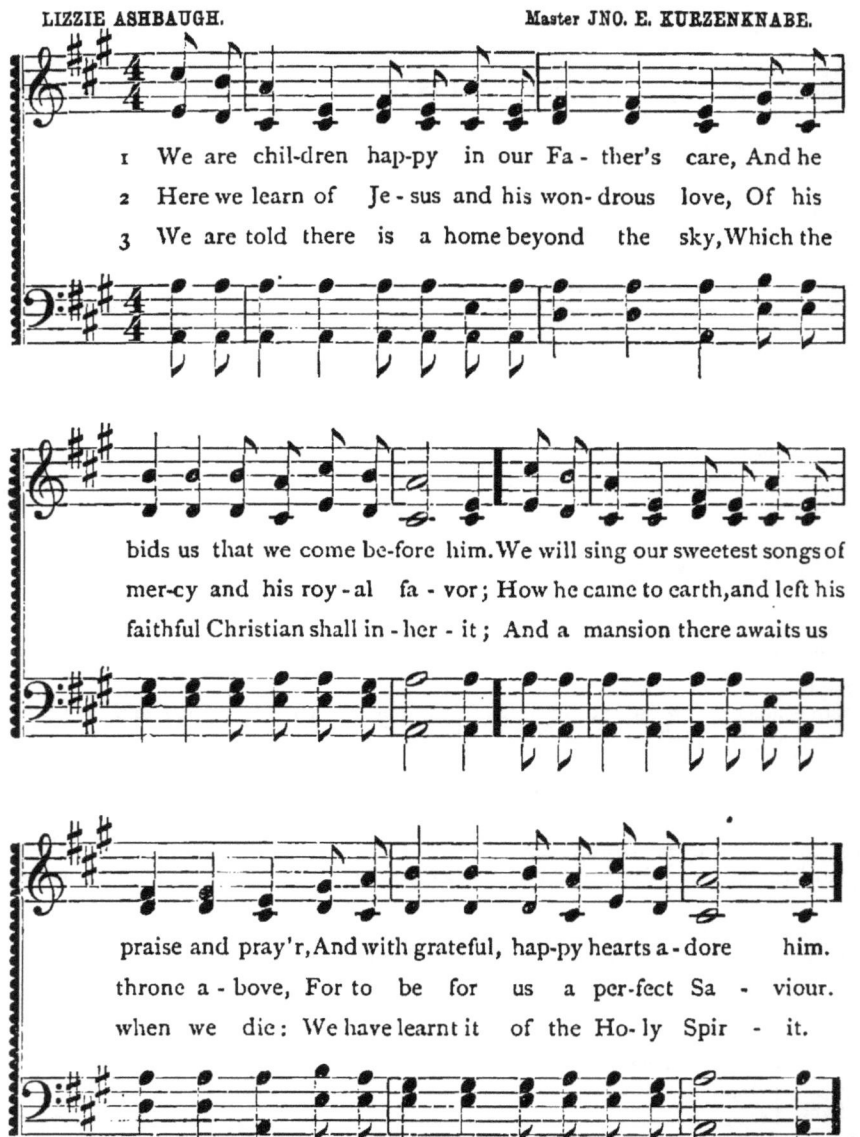

SWEETEST PRAISES NOW WE'LL SING.

SAFELY HIDE ME.

78. OUR SCHOOL FOR JESUS.
J. H. K.   J. H. KURZENKNABE.

Form in semicircle around altar. In second line of each verse use hand in following exercise:—VERSE 1.—Lift right hand. VERSE 2.—Point with index finger of right hand. VERSE 3.—Clasp hands, and kneel at "We humbly here." Rise in chorus.

1. Our school is all for Jesus; Our lifted hands we here employ To show that ev'ry girl and boy, With heart and hand can tes-ti-fy, That we are all for Jesus.

2. Our school is all for Jesus; We point to mansions in the sky, Where our most costly treasures lie, Where moth nor rust cannot destroy, For we are all for Jesus.

3. Our school is all for Jesus; With clasped hands in rev'rence now, We humbly here before him bow; And, one in Christ, re-peat the vow, That we are all for Jesus.

CHORUS.
Our whole school for Jesus, All for Jesus, all for Jesus.
Our whole school, all for Jesus.

Copyrighted by J. H. KURZENKNABE, A. D. 1880.

INDEX.

	PAGE
Accept the gift I bring	23
A home in heaven	36
All amiss do now forgive	55
Armor bearers	38
Brave Christian soldiers	49
Calling, gently calling	42
Canst thou tell?	56
Charity	66
Close to thee	13
Draw me nearer	10
Dear old story	65
Even me	26
Ever lead us by thy hand	32
Footsteps of Jesus	25
God is ever good	24
Good Shepherd, hear	75
Happy in the Lord	21
Happy is the man	79
Hear us, ever gracious Friend	33
He loveth the little ones	54
Hephzibah	37
Holy day of rest	46
I love the Sunday-school	9
I thank thee, Lord, for quiet rest	45
I will not let thee go	48
I will praise him in my youth	18
Jesus, the very thought of thee	61
Jesus, thou lovest me	72
Keep me safe, thou loving Friend	34
Let them come unto me	40
Life abundantly	44
Little armor bearers	38
Little pilgrims	5
Little things	17
Loving and praising our Jesus	43
Lullaby	73
Meek and lowly	14
My beloved	76

	PAGE
My Bible, oh, treasure divine	6
Nearer to thee, blessed Saviour	16
Never break the Sabbath	62
Oh, for a heart to praise	31
Oh, grant us now thy presence	27
Oh, I know a home awaits me	15
Oh, we are little workers	74
Oh, we are welcome	47
O treasure divine	6
Our school for Jesus	78
Over that Jasper Sea	50
Redeemed	8
Room in thine arms, dear Jesus	7
Safely hide me	70
Saviour, help us to give heed	39
Silvery echoes	4
Singing and working for Jesus	11
Singing for Jesus	20
Sing your sweetest carols	64
Stand up and bless the Lord	63
Sweetest praises now we'll sing	68
Take him at his word	57
Teach us more of thee	28
The Captain's band	58
The children's jubilee	51
The children's Saviour	60
The children's Shepherd	30
The dear old story	65
The happy land	41
The holy child Jesus	53
The holy day of rest	46
The little things	17
The Lord my Shepherd	22
Though I'm but a little child	12
Thou God of love and mercy, hear	29
We are coming, dearest Saviour	19
We are little armor bearers	38
We are little workers	74
We'll remember our Creator	35
We praise thee, Lord	3
We're a band of little children	28
We thank thee, Lord	45
Will you go?	52
Working for Jesus	11

J. M. ARMSTRONG & CO., Music Typographers, Philadelphia.

www.ingramcontent.com/pod-product-compliance
Lightning Source LLC
Chambersburg PA
CBHW020332090426
42735CB00009B/1499